The Church

What Am I Doing Here?

A four-week course to help people understand
the church.

by
Mike Nappa

Apply·It·To·Life™

Adult

BIBLE CURRICULUM
from Group

Group
Loveland, Colorado

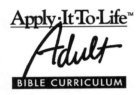

Group

The Church: What Am I Doing Here?
Copyright © 1995 Group Publishing, Inc.

This curriculum book is a significantly revised edition of a book by the same title, copyright © 1993 Group Publishing, Inc., Box 481, Loveland, CO 80539.

Credits
Editors: Stephen Parolini and Bob Buller
Senior Editor: Paul Woods
Creative Products Director: Joani Schultz
Art Director: Kathy Benson
Cover Designer: Liz Howe
Cover Illustrator: Dave Ross; The Stock Illustration Source, Inc.
Illustrator: Lisa Smith

ISBN 1-55945-513-6

10 9 8 7 6 5 4 3   04 03 02 01 00 99

Printed in the United States of America.

CONTENTS

Introduction

WHAT IS APPLY-IT-TO-LIFE™ ADULT BIBLE CURRICULUM?

Apply-It-To-Life™ Adult Bible Curriculum is a series of four-week study courses designed to help you facilitate powerful lessons that will help class members grow in faith. Use this course with
- Sunday school classes,
- home study groups,
- weekday Bible study groups,
- men's Bible studies,
- women's Bible studies, and
- family classes.

The variety of courses gives the adult student a broad coverage of topical, life-related issues and significant biblical topics. In addition, as the name of the series implies, every lesson helps the adult student apply Scripture to his or her life.

Each course in Apply-It-To-Life Adult Bible Curriculum provides four lessons on different aspects of one topic. In each course, you also receive Fellowship and Outreach Specials connected to the month's topic. They provide suggestions for building closer relationships in your class, outreach activities, and even a party idea!

WHAT MAKES APPLY-IT-TO-LIFE ADULT BIBLE CURRICULUM UNIQUE?

Teaching as Jesus Taught

Jesus was a master teacher. With Apply-It-To-Life Adult Bible Curriculum, you'll use the same teaching methods and principles that Jesus used:
- **Active Learning.** Think back on an important lesson you've learned in life. Did you learn it from reading about it? from hearing about it? from something you did? Chances are, the most important lessons you've learned came from something you experienced. That's what active learning is—learn-

ing by doing. Active learning leads students through activities and experiences that help them understand important principles, messages, and ideas. It's a discovery process that helps people internalize and remember what they learn.

Jesus often used active learning. One of the most vivid examples is his washing of his disciples' feet. In Apply-It-To-Life Adult Bible Curriculum, the teacher might remove his or her shoes and socks then read aloud the foot-washing passage from John 13, or the teacher might choose to actually wash people's feet. Participants won't soon forget it. Active learning uses simple activities to teach profound lessons.

● **Interactive Learning.** Interactive learning means learning through small-group interaction and discussion. While it may seem to be a simple concept, it's radically new to many churches that have stuck with a lecture format or large-group discussion for so long. With interactive learning, each person is actively involved in discovering God's truth through talking with other people about God's Word. Interactive learning is discussion with a difference. It puts people in pairs, trios, or foursomes to involve everyone in the learning experience. It takes active learning a step further by having people who have gone through an experience teach others what they've learned.

Jesus often helped cement the learning from an experience by questioning people—sometimes in small groups—about what had happened. He regularly questioned his followers and his opponents, forcing them to think and to discuss among themselves what he was teaching them. After washing his disciples' feet, the first thing Jesus did was ask the disciples if they understood what he had done. After the "foot washing" activity, the teacher might form small groups and have people discuss how they felt when the leader removed his or her shoes and socks. Then group members could compare those feelings and the learning involved to what the disciples must have experienced.

● **Biblical Depth.** Apply-It-To-Life Adult Bible Curriculum recognizes that most adults are ready to go below the surface to better understand the deeper truths of the Bible. Therefore, the activities and studies go beyond an "easy answer" approach to Christian education and lead adults to grapple with difficult issues from a biblical perspective.

Each lesson begins by giving the teacher resource material on the Bible passages covered in the study. In the Bible Basis, you'll find information that will help you understand the Scriptures you're dealing with. Within the class-time section of the lesson, thought-provoking activities and discussions lead adults to new depths of biblical understanding. Bible Insights within the lesson give pertinent information that will bring the

Bible to life for you and your class members. In-class handouts give adults significant Bible information and challenge them to search for and discover biblical truths for themselves. Finally, the "For Even Deeper Discussion" sections provide questions that will lead your class members to new and deeper levels of insight and application.

No one questions the depth of Jesus' teachings or the effectiveness of his teaching methods. This curriculum follows Jesus' example and helps people probe the depths of the Bible in a way no other adult curriculum does.

● **Bible Application.** Jesus didn't stop with helping people understand truth. For him, teaching took the learner beyond understanding to application. It wasn't enough that the rich young ruler knew all the right answers. Jesus wanted him to take action on what he knew. In the same way, Apply-It-To-Life Adult Bible Curriculum encourages a response in people's lives. That's why this curriculum is called "Apply-It-To-Life"! Depth of understanding means little if the truths of Scripture don't zing into people's hearts. Each lesson brings home one point and encourages people to consider the changes they might make in response.

● **One Purpose.** In each study, every activity works toward communicating and applying the same point. People may discover other new truths, but the study doesn't load them down with a mass of information. Sometimes less is more. When lessons try to teach too much, they often fail to teach anything. Even Jesus limited his teaching to what he felt people could really learn and apply (John 16:12). Apply-It-To-Life Adult Bible Curriculum makes sure that class members thoroughly understand and apply one point each week.

● **Variety.** People appreciate variety. Jesus constantly varied his teaching methods. One day he would have a serious discussion with his disciples about who he was and another day he'd baffle them by turning water into wine. What he didn't do was allow them to become bored with what he had to teach them.

Any kind of study can become less than exciting if the leader and students do everything the same way week after week. Apply-It-To-Life Adult Bible Curriculum varies activities and approaches to keep everyone's interest level high each week. In one class, you might have people in small groups "put themselves in the disciples' sandals" and experience something of the confusion of Jesus' death and resurrection. In another lesson, class members may experience problems in communication and examine how such problems can damage relationships.

To meet adults' varied needs, the courses cover a wide range of topics such as Jesus, knowing God's will, communication, taking faith to work, and highlights of Bible books. One month you may choose to study a family or personal faith issue; the next month you may cover a biblical topic such as the book of John.

● **Relevance.** People today want to know how to live successfully right now. They struggle with living as authentic Christians at work, in the family, and in the community. Most churchgoing adults want to learn about the Bible, but not merely for the sake of having greater Bible knowledge. They want to know how the Bible can help them live faithful lives—how it can help them face the difficulties of living in today's culture. Apply-It-To-Life Adult Bible Curriculum bridges the gap between biblical truth and the "real world" issues of people's lives. Jesus didn't discuss with his followers the eschatological significance of Ezekiel's wheels, and Apply-It-To-Life Adult Bible Curriculum won't either! Courses and studies in this curriculum focus on the real needs of people and help them discover answers in Scripture that will help meet those needs.

● **A Nonthreatening Atmosphere.** In many adult classes, people feel intimidated because they're new Christians or because they don't have the Bible knowledge they think they should have. Jesus sometimes intimidated those who opposed him, but he consistently treated his followers with understanding and respect. We want people in church to experience the same understanding and respect Jesus' followers experienced. With Apply-It-To-Life Adult Bible Curriculum, no one is embarrassed for not knowing or understanding as much as someone else. In fact, the interactive learning process minimizes the differences between those with vast Bible knowledge and those with little Bible knowledge. Lessons often begin with nonthreatening, sharing questions and move slowly toward more depth. Whatever their level of knowledge or commitment, class members will work together to discover biblical truths that can affect their lives.

● **A Group That Cares.** Jesus began his ministry by choosing a group of 12 people who learned from him together. That group practically lived together—sharing one another's hurts, joys, and ambitions. Sometimes Jesus divided the 12 into smaller groups and worked with just three or four at a time.

Studies have shown that many adults today long for a close-knit group of people with whom they can share personal needs and joys. And people interact more freely when they feel accepted in a group. Activities in this curriculum will help class members get to know one another better and care for one another more as they study the Bible and apply its truths to their lives. As people reveal their thoughts and feelings to one another, they'll grow closer and develop more commitment to the group and to each other. And they'll be encouraging one another along the way!

● **An Element of Delight.** We don't often think about Jesus' ministry in this way, but there certainly were times he brought fun and delight to his followers. Remember the time he raised Peter's mother-in-law? or the time he sat happily with children on his lap? How about the joy and excitement at his triumphal entry into Jerusalem? or the time he helped fishing disciples catch a boatload of fish—after they'd fished all night with no success?

People learn more when they're having fun. So within Apply-It-To-Life Adult Bible Curriculum, elements of fun and delight pop up often. And sometimes adding fun is as simple as using a carrot for a pretend microphone!

Taking the Fear out of Teaching

Teachers love Apply-It-To-Life Adult Bible Curriculum because it makes teaching much less stressful. Lessons in this curriculum

● **are easy to teach.** Interactive learning frees the teacher from being a dispenser of information to serve as a facilitator of learning. Teachers can spend class time guiding people to discover and apply biblical truths. The studies provide clear, understandable Bible background; easy-to-prepare learning experiences; and powerful, thought-provoking discussion questions.

● **can be prepared quickly.** Lessons in Apply-It-To-Life Adult Bible Curriculum are logical and clear. There's no sorting through tons of information to figure out the lesson. In 30 minutes, a busy teacher can easily read a lesson and prepare to teach it. In addition, optional and For Extra Time activities allow the teacher to tailor the lesson to the class. And the thorough instructions and questions will guide even an inexperienced teacher through each powerful lesson.

● **let everyone share in the class's success.** With Apply-It-To-Life Adult Bible Curriculum, the teacher is one of the participants. The teacher still guides the class, but the burden is not as heavy. Everyone participates and adds to the study's effectiveness. So when the study has an impact, everyone shares in that success.

● **lead the teacher to new discoveries.** Each lesson is designed to help the teacher first discover a biblical truth. And most teachers will make additional discoveries as they prepare each lesson. In class, the teacher will discover even more as other adults share what they have found. As with any type of teaching, the teacher will likely learn more than anyone else in the class!

● **provide relevant information to class members.**

Photocopiable handouts are designed to help people better understand or interpret Bible passages. And the handouts make teaching easier because the teacher can often refer to them for small-group discussion questions and instructions.

HOW TO USE APPLY-IT-TO-LIFE ADULT BIBLE CURRICULUM

First familiarize yourself with an Apply-It-To-Life Adult Bible Curriculum lesson. The following explanations will help you understand how the lesson elements work together.

Lesson Elements

● The **Opening** maps out the lesson's agenda and introduces your class to the topic for the session. Sometimes this activity will help people get better acquainted as they begin to explore the topic together.

● The **Bible Exploration and Application** activities will help people discover what the Bible says about the topic and how the lesson's point applies to their lives. In these varied activities, class members find answers to the "So what?" question. Through active and interactive learning methods, people will discover the relevance of the Scriptures and commit to growing closer to God.

You may use either one or both of the options in this section. They are designed to stand alone or to work together. Both present the same point in different ways. "For Even Deeper Discussion" questions appear at the end of each activity in this section. Use these questions whenever you feel they might be particularly helpful for your class.

● The **Closing** pulls everything in the lesson together and often funnels the lesson's message into a time of reflection and prayer.

● The **For Extra Time** section is just that. Use it when you've completed the lesson and still have time left or when you've used one Bible Exploration and Application option and don't have time to do the other. Or you might plan to use it instead of another option.

When you put all the sections together, you get a lesson that's fun and easy to teach. Plus, participants will learn truths they'll remember and apply to their daily lives.

About the Questions and Answers . . .

The answers given after discussion questions are responses participants *might* give. They aren't the only answers or the "right" answers. However, you can use them to spark discussion.

Real life doesn't always allow us to give the "right" answers. That's why some of the responses given are negative or controversial. If someone responds negatively, don't be shocked. Accept the person and use the opportunity to explore other perspectives on the issue.

To get more out of your discussions, use follow-up inquiries such as
- Tell me more.
- What do you mean by that?
- What makes you feel that way?

Guidelines for a Successful Adult Class

- **Be a facilitator, not a lecturer.** Apply-It-To-Life Adult Bible Curriculum is student-based rather than teacher-based. Your job is to direct the activities and facilitate the discussions. You become a choreographer of sorts: someone who gets everyone else involved in the discussion and keeps the discussion on track.

- **Teach adults how to form small groups.** Help adults discover the benefits of small-group discussions by assisting them in forming groups of four, three, or two—whatever the activity calls for. Small-group sharing allows for more discussion and involvement by all participants. It's not as threatening or scary to open up to two people as it would be to 20 or 200!

Some leaders decide not to form small groups because they want to hear everybody's ideas. The intention is good, but some people just won't talk in a large group. Use a "report back" time after small-group discussions to gather the best responses from all groups.

When you form small groups, don't always let people choose those right around them. Try creative group-forming methods to help everyone in the class get to know one another. For example, tell class members: Find three other people wearing the same color you are; choose two other people who like the same music you do; join three others who shop at the same grocery store you do; acquaint yourself with one person who was born the same month as you; find two people who like the same sports team as you; join three class members who like the same season as you, and so on. If you have fun with it, your class will, too!

● **Encourage relationship building.** George Barna, in his insightful book about the church, *The Frog in the Kettle,* explains that adults today have a strong need to develop friendships. In a society of high-tech toys, "personal" computers, and lonely commutes, people long for positive human contact. That's where our church classes and groups can jump in. Help adults form friendships through your class. What's discovered in a classroom setting will be better applied when friends support each other outside the classroom. In fact, the relationships begun in your class may be as important as the truths you help your adults learn.

● **Be flexible.** Sometimes your class will complete every activity in the lesson with great success and wonderful learning. But what should you do if people go off on a tangent? or they get stuck in one of the activities? What if you don't have time to finish the lesson?

Don't panic. People learn best when they are interested and engaged in meaningful discussion, when they move at their own pace. And if you get through even one activity, your class will discover the point for the whole lesson. So relax. It's OK if you don't get everything done. Try to get to the Closing in every lesson, since its purpose is to bring closure to the topic for the week. But if you don't, don't sweat it!

● **Expect the unexpected.** Active learning is an adventure that doesn't always take you where you think you're going. Don't be surprised if things don't go exactly the way you'd planned. Be open to the different directions the Holy Spirit may lead your class. When something goes wrong or an unexpected emotion is aroused, take advantage of this teachable moment. Ask probing questions; follow up on someone's deep need or concern. Those moments are often the best opportunities for learning that come our way.

● **Participate—and encourage participation.** Apply-It-To-Life Adult Bible Curriculum is only as interactive as you and your class make it. Learning arises out of dialogue. People need to grapple with and verbalize their questions and discoveries. Jump into discussions yourself, but don't "take over." Encourage everyone to participate. You can facilitate smooth discussions by using "active listening" responses such as rephrasing and summing up what's been said. If people seem stumped, use the possible responses after each question to spark further discussion. You may feel like a cheerleader at times, but your efforts will be worth it. The more people participate, the more they'll discover God's truths for themselves.

● **Trust the Holy Spirit.** All the previous six guidelines and the instructions in the lessons will be irrelevant if you ignore the presence of God in your classroom. God sent the Holy Spirit as our helper. As you use this curriculum, ask the Holy Spirit to help you facilitate the lessons. And ask the Holy Spirit to direct your class toward God's truth. Trust that God's Spirit can work through each person's discoveries, not just the teacher's.

How to Use This Course

Before the Four-Week Session
● Read the Course Introduction and This Course at a Glance (pp. 13-14).
● Decide how you'll use the art on the Publicity Page (p. 15) to publicize the course. Prepare fliers, newsletter articles, and posters as needed.
● Look at the Fellowship and Outreach Specials (pp. 63-64) and decide which ones you'll use.

Before Each Lesson
● Read the one-sentence Point, the Objectives, and the Bible Basis for the lesson. The Bible Basis provides background information on the lesson's passages and shows how those passages relate to people today.
● Choose which activities you'll use from the lesson. Remember, it's not important to do every activity. Pick the ones that best fit your group and time allotment.
● Gather necessary supplies. They're listed in This Lesson at a Glance.
● Read each section of the lesson. Adjust activities as necessary to fit your class size and meeting room, but be careful not to delete all the activity. People learn best when they're actively involved in the learning process.

COURSE INTRODUCTION— THE CHURCH: WHAT AM I DOING HERE?

"The church is full of hypocrites. I'll never go there."

"The church is out of touch with reality. Why waste my time?"

"I like the church until it interferes with my personal lifestyle."

"I'd love to get involved in church, but I just don't have time."

● ● ●

Sound familiar? Unfortunately Christians as well as non-Christians express these attitudes about church. But God never intended the church to be thought of as a boring, lifeless institution. The church—Christ's body—should be vibrant, alive, and life-changing.

Did you know...
● there are over 350,000 Protestant and Roman Catholic churches in the United States?
● 42 percent of American adults attend church once a week?
● 85 percent of American adults rate churches as a source of good influence on "the way things are going" in the United States?

But, did you know...
● 91 percent of non-Christians say churches are "not very sensitive" to their needs?
● 81 percent of Americans say they "can arrive at their own religious views without regard to a body of believers"?
● 53 percent of pastors say that "Christ would rate the church as having little positive impact on souls and society"?

When Jesus walked this earth, he said, "The Spirit of the Lord is on me, because he has anointed me to preach good news to the poor. He has sent me to proclaim freedom for the prisoners and recovery of sight for the blind, to release the oppressed, to proclaim the year of the Lord's favor" (Luke 4:18-19, New International Version).

Jesus lived out this passage and changed the world forever. The same Spirit that filled Jesus now fills his body, the church. In addition, the Holy Spirit empowers Christians today to live out Jesus' work in new and creative ways. As members of the body of Christ, we too can change the world for Christ's sake.

Explore these four lessons with your class to discover how the Holy Spirit's power can make your home church a vibrant, alive, and life-changing place.

This Course at a Glance

Before you dive into the lessons, familiarize yourself with each lesson's point. Then read the Scripture passages.

- Study them as a background to the lessons.
- Use them as a basis for your personal devotions.
- Think about how they relate to people's situations today.

Lesson 1: In the Beginning
The Point: The church finds its life and power in the Holy Spirit.
Bible Basis: Acts 2:1-21, 37-47

Lesson 2: A Healthy Balance
The Point: Healthy churches balance worship, instruction, community, and outreach.
Bible Basis: Acts 2:42-47

Lesson 3: Together We Stand
The Point: Everyone contributes something important to the church.
Bible Basis: Romans 12:3-8 and 1 Corinthians 12:12-26

Lesson 4: Divided We Fall
The Point: God can help us resolve conflict in a positive way.
Bible Basis: Acts 15:1-21 and Galatians 5:13-15

Grab your congregation's attention! Add the vital details to the ready-made flier below, photocopy it, and use it to advertise this course on the church. Insert the flier into your bulletins. Enlarge it to make posters. Splash the art or anything else from this page onto newsletters, bulletins, or even postcards! It's that simple.

*The art from this page is also available on Group's MinistryNet™ computer on-line resource for you to manipulate on your computer. Call **800-447-1070** for information.*

THE CHURCH: WHAT AM I DOING HERE?

A four-week adult course on the church and every Christian's place in it.

COME TO

ON

AT

COME LEARN ABOUT YOUR ROLE IN THE BODY OF BELIEVERS!

THE CHURCH: WHAT AM I DOING HERE?

THE CHURCH: WHAT AM I DOING HERE?

In the Beginning

The church finds its life and power in the Holy Spirit.

◀ THE POINT

OBJECTIVES

Participants will
- examine what it might have been like to be present during the birth of the church,
- discuss how the Holy Spirit has been and should be active in the church, and
- compare the early church to the church today.

BIBLE BASIS

Read the Scripture for this lesson. Then read the following background paragraphs to see how the passage relates to people today.

Acts 2:1-21, 37-47 records the birth of the church on the day of Pentecost.

ACTS 2:1-21, 37-47

Jesus' disciples didn't want him to leave this earth, but when his personal ministry was complete, they were to continue his work. During the 40 days following his resurrection, Jesus taught them about the kingdom of God and its advancement. Then, before he ascended back to the Father (Acts 1:3-11), he left them with the promise that the Holy Spirit would help them spread news about him throughout the entire world.

Jesus fulfilled that promise on the day of Pentecost, a Jewish feast observed on the 50th day after the Passover Sabbath (49 days after Jesus' resurrection). The Holy Spirit descended on 120 followers of Jesus and filled them with the same power that had raised Jesus from the dead. In a single moment, the church was born. Before the day was over, the church would consist of more than 3,000 members.

Several unusual signs marked the coming of the Holy Spirit. First the gathered believers heard the sound of a violent wind. Then "tongues" of fire appeared above each person. The tonguelike shape of the fire may have symbolized the gift of tongues that was soon to follow, while the fire itself probably symbolized God's presence (see Exodus 3:2-6; Luke 3:16). Finally, the Holy Spirit filled Jesus' followers, and they declared the wonders of God in languages that everyone could understand. It was as though God had temporarily reversed the confusion of languages that had plagued humanity since the tower of Babel (see Genesis 11:1-9).

Devout Jews from many countries had gathered in Jerusalem for the feast of Pentecost. When they heard these Spirit-filled Galileans speaking languages other than the commonly known Aramaic or Greek, they knew that something noteworthy was taking place. They simply didn't know what it was or what it meant. As always, however, there were skeptics in the crowd. They concluded that Jesus' followers were drunk.

Against this background, Peter stood up and addressed the large crowd that had gathered. After humorously dismissing the charge of drunkenness—it was too early in the morning to be drunk!—Peter explained that what people were seeing was nothing less than the fulfillment of Joel's prophecy that God would pour out his Spirit on all people (Joel 2:28-32).

Peter went on to demonstrate that Jesus, whom the Jews had rejected less than two months earlier, provided forgiveness of sins. Although Jesus had performed miracles, signs, and wonders among them, they had killed him. However, Jesus was risen from the dead and exalted to the position of Lord and Messiah, making forgiveness and the gift of the Spirit available to all.

Peter's words so pierced the hearts of his listeners that they interrupted him to ask what to do. Peter told them to repent and be baptized as an outward sign of their repentance. If they would do that, they, too, would receive the Holy Spirit. Incredibly, some 3,000 people responded. In a single day, more people became followers of Jesus than during Jesus' entire ministry.

It's important to recognize that the church began not with an organizational meeting, but as a work of God's Spirit. Organization was secondary. Still, the new community needed some order, so they united around the apostles' teaching, worshiped and prayed to God together, and shared their meals and possessions. The outcome pleased God, the church enjoyed the favor of everyone, and God added new converts every day.

On the day of Pentecost, the Holy Spirit came to Christians who had dedicated themselves to seek and pray for God's will. When today's church seeks God's will, the

Holy Spirit also enables it to continue the plan God started with the early church at Pentecost. Now, as then, the Holy Spirit can turn any group of Christians into a dynamic, world-changing force. Use this lesson to help your class members experience the power of the Holy Spirit in their lives and in your church.

THIS LESSON AT A GLANCE

Section	Minutes	What Participants Will Do	Supplies
OPENING	up to 10	**HOLIDAY HELLOS**—Tell each other their favorite holidays.	Cupcakes
BIBLE EXPLORATION AND APPLICATION	20 to 30	☐ Option 1: **DIARY IMAGINATIONS**—Illustrate the events recorded in Acts 2:1-21 and write fictitious diary entries from the perspectives of people at Pentecost.	Bibles, paper, pencils
	15 to 25	☐ Option 2: **THAT WAS THEN, THIS IS NOW**—Compare the church today to the early church described in Acts 2:1-4, 37-47.	Bibles, paper, pencils, newsprint, tape, marker
CLOSING	up to 5	**SILENT PRAYER WALK**—Mentally "walk" through the church's ministries and pray for the Holy Spirit's leading in them.	
FOR EXTRA TIME	up to 10	**Church Affirmations**—Discuss how their church has and could affect their community.	
	up to 10	**No Church?**—Imagine how the world would be different if there were no church.	

Holiday Hellos

(up to 10 minutes)

As you begin the class, thank class members for attending and tell them what you'll be learning in today's lesson. Use the following statement or your own summary of the point: **Welcome to the first week of our study of the church. During the next four weeks, we'll answer questions such as "How did the church begin?" "What makes a good church?" "What's my role in the church?" and "How can we resolve conflict?" Today we're going to explore how  the church finds its life and power in the Holy Spirit.**

Throughout this course, we'll be doing things you might not expect in an adult class. We'll spend time on projects and in small-group discussions. We'll have some fun while we're challenged to learn. I look forward to all of us making this class unforgettable.

Form a circle and say: **To begin, let's learn a little about each other. Starting with the person on my left, take turns answering this question: Which is your favorite holiday and why?**

Give everyone a moment to think, then begin the discussion time. After everyone has had a chance to answer, say: **Holidays are some of the most important days of the year, but there's one holiday Christians often overlook—Pentecost, the day the church was born.**

Serve cupcakes (or another popular treat) for everyone to enjoy in honor of the church's birthday.

As group members enjoy their refreshments, say: **Today, we're going to begin our series on the church by examining what happened many years ago on the Jewish feast day called Pentecost and discovering how those events still affect our lives today.**

Lead the group in a prayer such as this: **Lord, we're thankful that ▷ the church finds its life and power in the Holy Spirit. Guide us as we examine Scripture to learn about the birth of the church and what it means to us today.**

THE POINT ▷

TEACHER
TIP

If you have more than eight class members, form groups of eight or fewer and have groups do this activity at the same time. Also, if your meeting room isn't big enough to form circles, have adults group together in the best way they can so each person can see the other members of his or her group.

THE POINT ▷

☐ **OPTION 1:**
Diary Imaginations

(20 to 30 minutes)

Say: **It must have been an exciting and unusual experience to be pre-**

sent when the church was born. Let's picture what that might have been like.

Ask two volunteers to read the Scripture aloud. Have the first volunteer read **Acts 2:1-12** and the second read **Acts 2:13-21.** As they read, have other class members imagine the entire scene: the place, the people, the smells, the sounds, and so on.

Give each person a sheet of paper and a pencil. Instruct class members to imagine themselves as part of the biblical scene then draw pictures of it. The illustrations can be either simple or complex, but they should somehow portray what happened at Pentecost.

After several minutes, form groups of four. Instruct group members to explain their drawings to each other. Then have the groups discuss the following questions. Ask:

● **What was it like to illustrate the events of Pentecost?** (It was frustrating because there was too much going on; it helped me focus on the key events; it made me realize just how odd the scene must have looked.)

● **How might your reactions to drawing Pentecost be like the reactions of people who were there? How might they be different?** (They were probably as confused as I am; there was probably too much to take in; we're better able to control what's going on.)

● **What was the most impressive sign of the Holy Spirit?** (The ability to speak in other languages; Peter's courage to preach to the crowd; the wind and the tongues of fire.)

● **What would you have liked most about being present at the coming of the Holy Spirit? What would you have liked least?** (I would have liked seeing a demonstration of God's power; I would've liked seeing the Spirit at work; I would've been uncomfortable with the confusion.)

● **How would you have reacted if you had been filled with the Holy Spirit as they were? if you had been an onlooker?** (I would've liked the sense of power; I would've fought to maintain control of myself; I've seen too many frauds, so I would've been skeptical.)

Ask the groups to report any insightful answers with the rest of the class. After each group has reported, distribute paper and pencils to everyone. Give group members several minutes to work together to write a brief, one-paragraph diary entry using the perspective of someone present during the events of **Acts 2:1-21.** Have each member of the group copy the diary entry.

Then have everyone create different foursomes with at least two new people. Direct these group members to share their diary entries with each other. After several minutes,

The Holy Spirit is the third person of the Trinity. In the Old Testament, the Holy Spirit temporarily came upon select people so they could perform specific tasks. However, Jesus promised that, after he returned to the Father, the Holy Spirit would come and live within every Christian. The coming of the Holy Spirit on the day of Pentecost fulfilled that promise. Now the Holy Spirit lives within all Christians and helps them overcome sin, enables them to serve others, and provides a direct link with God.

TEACHER

To make sure the class considers several perspectives, you may want to assign different roles—a disciple, an awed listener, a skeptic, Peter—to different groups.

have groups discuss the following questions one at a time then report their groups' responses to the whole class. Ask:

● **What did you learn from the diary entries?** (Some people were skeptical because it seemed too much like a trick; being filled with the Spirit like that would have been a life-changing experience; I'd have believed when I heard people speaking in my own language.)

● **Why is Pentecost regarded as the time the church was born?** (That's when the Holy Spirit empowered Jesus' followers to continue his ministry; that's when Jesus' followers organized into a distinct group without Jesus being there physically.)

● **Why did God choose to begin the church by sending the Holy Spirit?** (God wanted to start the church in a dynamic way; God wanted Christ's followers to experience the power of their faith.)

● **How does this relate to the way we establish new churches today? How is it different?** (We ask the Holy Spirit to help us reach out to others; we rely on the Spirit's enabling and guidance; we rely more on our own abilities than on God's power.)

● **How have you seen the Holy Spirit work in the church today?** (The Holy Spirit changes peoples' lives; people serve each other by exercising the gifts of the Spirit; the Holy Spirit makes our worship meaningful.)

● **What other ways should we see the Holy Spirit at work?** (We should see the gifts of the Spirit more than we do; we could be just as courageous as Peter was.)

Say: **Sometimes it's easy to lose our perspective and think of the church only in terms of buildings, planning sessions, and Sunday school programs. When that happens, we need to remember that ▶ the church finds its life and power in the Holy Spirit. On the day of Pentecost, the Holy Spirit turned a group of confused, frightened Christians into a dynamic force that changed the world. If we are open to God's leading, the Holy Spirit can and will do the same for us today.**

BIBLE INSIGHT

Luke, the author of Acts, indicates that Pentecost was the beginning of the church in several ways. First, in Acts 2:2 he uses an unusual Greek word for "wind" *(pnoē)* that is elsewhere used for the *creative* breath of God (Acts 17:25). Luke also refers to the coming of the Spirit as "the beginning" (Acts 11:15-16).

THE POINT ▶

■ ■

FOR *Even Deeper* DISCUSSION

Form groups of four or fewer and discuss the following questions:

● Why were some people amazed and others skeptical when the early believers spoke in tongues? Were their experiences different? Did they interpret the same experience differently?

● How is the gift of tongues described in Acts 2:1-13 like

the gift Paul discusses in 1 Corinthians 14? How is it different? To what extent should today's church practice this gift?

■ ■

☐ **O P T I O N 2 :**

That Was Then, This Is Now

(15 to 20 minutes)

Have adults re-form their original groups of four from the previous activity (or form new groups of four if you didn't do the previous activity). Give each group two sheets of paper and a pencil.

Direct each foursome to assign the following roles within its group: a scribe who will record the group's ideas, a reader who will read the Scriptures for the group, a representative who will share the group's findings with everyone else, and an encourager who will lead the discussion and urge all group members to participate.

Say: **In your groups, brainstorm words or phrases that describe the church today. You may want to describe what the church is, what the church does, what keeps the church going, why the church exists, and things like that. Be honest; not everything about the church today is positive. The scribes will write your ideas on one of your sheets of paper.**

Give groups several minutes to list descriptive words and phrases. While groups work, tape two sheets of newsprint to the wall. Label one sheet of newsprint "The Church Today" and the other "The Early Church."

After several minutes, ask representatives from the groups to share their groups' ideas. Using a marker, write these ideas on the newsprint labeled "The Church Today."

Then have the reader in each group read **Acts 2:1-4, 37-47** aloud. Give groups several minutes to brainstorm at least five words or phrases that characterize the early church as it is described in the verses. Have the scribes record their groups' ideas on the second sheet of paper. Afterward, have representatives share these new descriptions with the rest of the class. Write these ideas on the newsprint labeled "The Early Church."

Then have groups discuss the following questions. Pause after each question to allow time for discussion and encourage volunteers to share their groups' responses with the entire class. Ask:

● **What thoughts run through your mind as you compare these two lists?** (I'm disappointed because our lists are so different; I'm pleased because the lists are generally similar; I'm curious why we described the church today differently than the early church.)

● **In what ways are the two descriptions alike? How are they different?** (Both include prayer; both include learning about God; only one lists "sharing resources"; the church today is described as "out of touch with the world.")

● **Why are there differences between the early church and the church today?** (We rely more on committees and programs than on the Holy Spirit; we live in a radically different society; we've forgotten our roots; we've become too bound to tradition.)

● **What can we do to make these lists more alike?** (We can pray together more honestly and more often; we can ask God for a renewal of the Holy Spirit in our church; we can explore new ways to meet each other's needs; we can open our homes to each other.)

● **What role will the Holy Spirit play in this?** (The Holy Spirit will guide us to the truth; the Holy Spirit will give us strength to stand strong in the midst of strife; the Holy Spirit will unify us in God's work.)

T H E   P O I N T▷

Say: ▷**The Christian church finds its life and power in the Holy Spirit. When the Spirit came on Pentecost, thousands of lives radically changed. We have access to the Holy Spirit's power in the church today. Let's take advantage of that power to change lives in our church this week.**

■ ■

FOR *Even Deeper*
DISCUSSION

Form groups of four or fewer and discuss the following questions:

● To what extent should the church today be characterized by all of the things described in Acts 2:1-4, 37-47? What other ways can the church today evidence the working of the Holy Spirit?

● The early church enjoyed favor with all people (Acts 2:47). Does today's church enjoy the favor of others? Why or why not? How can the church increase its favor with those outside of the church?

■ ■

APPLY ■ IT ■ TO
LIFE
THIS WEEK

The "Apply-It-To-Life This Week" handout (p. 26) helps people further explore the issues uncovered in today's class. Give everyone a photocopy of the handout. Encourage class members to take time during the coming week to explore the questions and activities listed on the handout.

Silent Prayer Walk

(up to 5 minutes)

Say: ▶ **We the church find our life and power in the Holy Spirit. One of the best ways to tap into the Holy Spirit's power is to pray for it. Let's close today by mentally "walking" through our church and silently praying for its ministries. As I name a ministry, silently ask God for the Holy Spirit's working in that area.**

Name as many of your church's ministries as time permits, pausing for 20 seconds after each one. For example, you could name ministries to infants, children, youth, adults, single parents, the homeless, troubled families, people outside of the church, and so on. After you have named the pertinent areas, say: **Now ask God to show you where he wants you to fit into our church or into one of these ministries.** After one minute, close in prayer.

 For Extra Time

CHURCH AFFIRMATIONS

(up to 10 minutes)

Form groups of five. Have groups discuss the influence your church has in your community through organized programs or through the efforts of individuals and groups within the church. Ask class members to share stories about how the church has made a difference in people's lives, including their own. Then discuss what people in the community seem to think of the church and what each member could do to improve church–community relations.

NO CHURCH?

(up to 10 minutes)

Form trios. Instruct trios to imagine what the world would be like if the church had never been formed. Have trios come up with descriptions of this "churchless" world and explain them to the rest of the group. Then ask class members to brainstorm positive results of having the church in the world.

In the Beginning

The Point: ▶ The church finds its life and power in the Holy Spirit.

Scripture Focus: Acts 2:1-21, 37-47

Reflecting on God's Word

Each day this week, read one of the following Scriptures and examine what that passage says about the church. Then examine how well you are applying the message of that passage to your life. List your discoveries in the space under each passage.

Day 1: Colossians 1:18. Christ is the head of the church, which is his body.

Day 2: Ephesians 5:25-27. Christ gave himself for the church to make it perfect.

Day 3: Matthew 16:15-18. No power can keep the church from being victorious.

Day 4: Galatians 3:26-29. True equality is found only in Christ.

Day 5: Ephesians 4:1-6. We should maintain the unity of the Spirit.

Day 6: Psalm 122:1. Gathering with other believers is cause for joy.

> "Culture is most profoundly changed not by the efforts of huge institutions but by individual people being changed."—Charles W. Colson

---

Beyond Reflection

1. Interview five people this week by reading them Charles Colson's statement and asking whether or not they agree with it. Encourage them to support their opinions with specific examples. Then ask yourself these questions:
   ● Do you agree or disagree with Charles Colson's statement? Why?
   ● In what ways does the church change modern culture one person at a time?
   ● If you could change today's culture in one way, what would you change? How can you begin that change this week?

2. Discover that the church is more than just a building by visiting your church meeting place when no one is present. (You may need permission if you're visiting at an odd hour.)

Prayerfully walk through the sanctuary, into the fellowship room, down the hallways, and into the Sunday school classrooms. Compare your experience in the empty facilities to your experience when believers are joined together there.

Before you leave, pause and offer a prayer of thanks to God for the people of your church.

Next Week's Bible Passage: Acts 2:42-47

A Healthy Balance

Healthy churches balance worship, instruction, community, and outreach.

◀ **THE POINT**

OBJECTIVES

Participants will
- research the elements of worship, instruction, community, and outreach;
- lead each other in worship, instruction, community, and outreach activities; and
- diagram how to balance the elements of worship, instruction, community, and outreach.

BIBLE BASIS

Look up the Scripture for this lesson. Then read the following background paragraphs to see how the passage relates to people today.

In **Acts 2:42-47,** Luke describes the life and growth of the early church at Jerusalem.

ACTS 2:42-47

When 3,000 people responded to Peter's sermon at Pentecost, they immediately formed the first church. Organizing such a large number of people from diverse backgrounds was no small task. But under the enabling and guidance of the Holy Spirit, this body of believers soon became a unified, dynamic witness for Christ. Even after many returned to their homelands, the church continued to grow. To a great extent, the church succeeded because it balanced worship, instruction, community, and outreach—the key elements of healthy church life.

According to Acts 2:42-47, the Jerusalem church worshiped in various ways, including praying, gathering in the temple courts, and praising God together. But it's almost certain that the early church honored God in other ways as well. Like the ancient Israelites, the church talked and sang about God's good character and deeds (Psalm 113). In addition, the early Christians probably dedicated themselves to God and to true spiritual worship (Romans 12:1; John 4:23-24).

Instruction receives the least emphasis in Acts 2:42-47. However, many of the new Christians would have known little about Jesus, so the apostles presumably passed on Jesus' teachings and explained his life, death, and resurrection. Also, the church probably searched the Old Testament to learn more about God's workings in history and God's will for their lives (2 Timothy 3:16–4:2; Deuteronomy 6:4-9). Finally, church members taught each other what the Holy Spirit had revealed to them either through God's Word or through direct revelation (John 14:26; Colossians 3:16).

The most striking characteristic of the Jerusalem church was its sense of community. These people shared everything: their lives, their meals, even their possessions. In fact, many sold real estate (possessions—translated from Greek *ktēmata*) or other personal property (goods—translated from Greek *hyparxeis*) to meet the needs of others. In every possible way, the early Christians entered into one another's lives and met each other's physical and spiritual needs (Romans 12:9-16; Galatians 6:2; James 5:13-16). Consequently, they developed the camaraderie and unity that God wants in the church (Ephesians 2:13-22).

For all their concern for each other, the early Christians didn't neglect people outside the church. Likewise, the Holy Spirit didn't stop working after the day of Pentecost. The apostles continued to perform miracles, and the rest of the church enjoyed favor with the people. As a result, God brought new Christians into the community every day. Of course, it's likely that the church contributed to good relations by talking about and demonstrating God's love at every opportunity (Acts 1:8; Galatians 6:9-10; James 1:26-27; 1 Peter 3:15-16).

The early church at Jerusalem was in a unique (and enviable) position. After receiving an amazing outpouring of God's Spirit, it had the opportunity to start something completely new. Generally speaking, the church today seems to have lost the freshness and immediacy of the Spirit that made the early church so dynamic. Yet even today—2,000 years later—believers can still experience the joy of being part of a church that's actively led by the Spirit. Use this lesson to help your class balance worship, instruction, community, and outreach in the church today.

Section	Minutes	What Participants Will Do	Supplies
OPENING	up to 10	**PIE CHART CHURCHES**—Create pie charts that show what they think churches should do.	Paper plates, pencils, tape, newsprint, marker
BIBLE EXPLORATION AND APPLICATION	20 to 30	☐ Option 1: **COMMITTEE RESEARCH**—Serve on church planning committees and learn the characteristics of worship, instruction, community, and outreach from various Scriptures.	Bibles, "Planning-Committee Scriptures" handout (p. 37), newsprint, marker, paper, pencils
	15 to 20	☐ Option 2: **EIGHT-MINUTE CHURCHES**—Lead each other in acting out the four elements of a healthy church and discuss Acts 2:42-47.	
CLOSING	up to 5	**TAKING IT HOME**—Pray for each other and commit to phoning each other at least once during the coming week.	
FOR EXTRA TIME	up to 10	**CHURCH PLANTING**—Plan churches that balance worship, instruction, community, and outreach.	Paper, pencils
	up to 10	**HERE AT HOME**—Evaluate how well their church programs balance worship, instruction, community, and outreach.	Newsprint, marker

Pie Chart Churches

(up to 10 minutes)

You may want to define the four elements and give a few examples of each one. For instance, you could define worship as "telling God how much we appreciate him" and explain that people often worship by praying to God or singing about God.

If you have more than eight in your class, form groups of eight or fewer and have groups discuss the questions.

THE POINT ▷

To begin this lesson, give everyone a paper plate and a pencil. Tape a piece of newsprint to the wall.

Say: **People come to church for a number of different reasons. Why do you think people attend church? As you call out your ideas, I'll write them down.**

Have the class members call out their ideas while you list them on the newsprint. After a moment or two, summarize the reasons for church attendance by writing worship, instruction, community, and outreach, then circle those four elements for easy reference. Say: **Since people attend church for worship, instruction, community, and outreach, it's hard to know how much emphasis we should place on each reason or element. On the front of your paper plate, draw a pie chart that represents how you think our church divides its energies between these four elements. For example, if you think we spend 50 percent of our time and energy on worship, label half your pie chart "worship." You have one minute. Go.**

When they are finished, ask class members to take turns explaining their pie charts. Allow people to pass if others have already shared similar percentages.

Then instruct class members to turn their plates over and make new pie charts. These will represent the way they think your church *should* divide its efforts between worship, instruction, community, and outreach.

After one minute, have each person compare his or her charts. Ask:

● **How does your ideal church compare with our actual church?** Answers will vary.

● **What accounts for the similarities between your pie charts? What accounts for the differences?** (Our church takes time for all of these elements; I have personal needs that others in the church don't feel; I'm a new Christian, so I want to learn as much as I can.)

● **How do our personal interests affect the focus of our church?** (If we're excited about one area, we lead others in that direction; we expect others to see the same needs that we do; we associate with people who are just like us, and the church becomes unbalanced.)

Say: **Today we're going to explore how▷ a healthy church balances worship, instruction, community, and outreach. As we explore these four elements, think about how they apply to you as a member of this church and as a member of the larger body of Christ.**

☐ OPTION 1:
Committee Research
(20 to 30 minutes)

Before class, photocopy the "Planning-Committee Scriptures" handout (p. 37) and cut apart the sections. If you have more than 20 in your class, make one copy for every 20 persons. On a sheet of newsprint, draw a large pie chart similar to the one in the margin.

Ask a volunteer to read **Acts 2:42-47** aloud. Then have class members assign the activities described in these verses to one or more of the categories on the pie chart. Write their suggestions in the appropriate sections of the chart. Say: **From the very start, God wanted▶ churches to balance worship, instruction, community, and outreach. That's what we see in the early church, and it's what we should see today. But that doesn't mean we have to do everything the same way the early church did. In fact, it's far more important to understand what worship, instruction, community, and outreach really are than to perform tired, old rituals simply out of habit.**

Form four groups and have each group choose a recorder. Give each recorder a section of the "Planning-Committee Scriptures" handout and a pencil.

Say: **Each of you has just been assigned to a church planning committee. Each committee is to prepare a report that explains the characteristics of its assigned topic. One group will be the worship committee, another will be in charge of instruction, and so on.**

Use the Scriptures on the handout and any others you know to prepare your report. For example, since Acts 2:46 records that early church members ate together, the community group could list "eating together" as a characteristic of community in a church.

Have your recorder list your group's insights on the handout. In 10 minutes we'll ask a representative from each group to report that committee's findings.

After eight minutes, warn groups to start summarizing their thoughts. When the time is up, instruct each group to select the person who lives farthest from the church to act as its representative. Have representatives take turns sharing their groups' descriptions of their assigned elements. Record groups' findings in the appropriate sections of the diagram on your newsprint.

Then instruct people to number off within their church planning committees. Gather the ones into a new four-

◀ **THE POINT**

TEACHER

If you have more than 20 in your class, form groups of five or fewer and assign the same category (worship, instruction, community, or outreach) to different groups.

some, the twos into another, and so on. Each new group should have one member from each of the four church planning committees. Have group members discuss the following questions one at a time. After each discussion, invite volunteers to report their groups' responses. Ask:

● **What impressed you the most about the committee reports?** (The Bible has a lot to say about community; we've just scratched the surface of understanding worship; each of the elements is vital.)

● **Why does the Bible place so much emphasis on worship? on instruction? on community? on outreach?** (Worship reminds us of God's goodness; instruction helps us understand God, the world, and ourselves; community meets the basic human need to be with other people; in outreach, we tell non-Christians about God's love.)

● **What happens when a church functions well in each of these areas?** (It pleases and honors God; its people grow closer to God and to one another; others are attracted to it.)

● **What happens when a church doesn't function well in one or more of these areas?** (It becomes stagnant; it starts to focus more on programs and less on God; its people don't mature in a healthy way.)

● **How well does our church match the biblical description of worship? of instruction? of community? of outreach?** (Our worship is not as meaningful as it should be; we've erected too many walls between ourselves and the world; our Christian education program is solid.)

● **What could we do to improve in these four areas?** (We need a better balance between worship and instruction; we could encourage community by starting small groups; we need to try harder to have good relations with people in the community.)

Say: **One way to measure a church's health is to see how well it balances worship, instruction, community, and outreach. Although we may gauge our success by the number of people who attend our church or the size of our church budget, God's standard is different. According to God, ▷ healthy churches are churches that maintain a good balance between worship, instruction, community, and outreach.**

THE POINT ▷

■■■■■■■■■■■■■■■■■■■■■■■■■■■

FOR *Even Deeper* DISCUSSION

Form groups of four or fewer and discuss the following questions:

● To what extent should the church change to accommodate different needs and situations? For example, should church members share all of their possessions? live together? meet daily? Should we modify or expand the apostles' teaching? Explain.

● How actively should the church seek favor with those outside of the church? How can the church oppose sin in the society without alienating members of society?

■■■■■■■■■■■■■■■■■■■■■■■■■■■

☐ **OPTION 2:**

Eight-Minute Churches

(15 to 20 minutes)

Form groups of four (or keep the same groups from the previous activity). Have members within each group select one person to study worship, one to study instruction, one community, and one outreach. Send worship group members to one area of the room, instruction group members to another, and so on.

Say: **Since ▶ a healthy church balances worship, instruction, community, and outreach, let's practice those things right now by doing an exercise called Eight-Minute Churches.**

Tell the new groups they have five minutes to prepare a two-minute activity they can lead in their original foursomes. For example, the worship group might practice a worship song. The instruction group might choose a biblical passage and brainstorm insights to share with others. The community group might think of a way to encourage others. The outreach group might decide to pray for non-Christian friends.

After five minutes, re-form the original groups of four and have them spread out around the room. Starting with those who studied worship, give each group member two minutes to lead the rest of the group in his or her selected activity.

When everyone is finished, have those who studied instruction read **Acts 2:42-47** to their groups and discuss the following questions together one at a time. After each discussion, ask volunteers to take turns reporting their groups' answers. Ask:

● **What was it like to lead an activity?** (I felt uncomfortable, because I'm not used to teaching others; I was encouraged, because it was good to see us all acting out

TEACHER TIP

If you have more than 24 members in your class, divide the worship, instruction, community, and outreach groups into smaller groups of at least three people each for this activity.

◀ **THE POINT**

TEACHER TIP

If the class did not complete "Committee Research," instruct groups to read Acts 2:42-47 then write brief descriptions of their assigned elements. Allow several additional minutes for groups to do this.

what we're learning; we were pressed for time.)

● **How does this exercise compare with the experience of the people in Acts 2:42-47?** (The activity made us rely on the Holy Spirit as they did; we imitated the attitudes and actions of the people in this Scripture; we had only a shallow experience, while theirs was in-depth.)

● **In what ways do you see our church following the example of Acts 2:42-47?** (We take time to pray; we concentrate on learning the apostles' teaching; we share with each other; we experience joy as the early Christians did.)

● **What helps you worship? learn about God? feel a sense of community? reach out to others?** (Music inspires me; I learn best when I study the Bible for myself; I feel like part of a community when others take interest in my personal life; seeing positive examples of leaders in our church makes me want to reach out to others.)

● **In which of these areas—worship, instruction, community, or outreach—would you most like to improve? Why?** (Worship, because I need to show my love for God more; instruction, because sometimes I believe things that aren't true; community, because I'm afraid to open up to others; outreach, because I'm uncomfortable talking about my faith.)

● **What can we do to help each other improve in these areas?** (Pray for each other; tell each other when God does something good in our lives; share what we learn from our personal study with each other; practice talking about our faith with each other.)

Say: **We can have the same satisfying church experience today that the early church had nearly 2,000 years ago. To do so, we need to make sure that we ▷ develop and balance the essential elements of a healthy church: worship, instruction, community, and outreach.**

T H E　P O I N T ▷

■■■■■■■■■■■■■■■■■■■■■■■■■■

FOR *Even Deeper* **DISCUSSION**

Form groups of four or fewer and discuss the following questions:

● Are there other elements besides the four we've discussed that are essential to a healthy church life? If so, what are they? Why do you think they are essential?

● Are any of the four elements more important than the others? Explain. To what extent should we emphasize specific elements to adjust to different situations?

● Are there any absolutes of healthy church life? If so, what are they?

■■■■■■■■■■■■■■■■■■■■■■■■■■

APPLY·IT·TO LIFE THIS WEEK The "Apply-It-To-Life This Week" handout (p. 38) helps people further explore the issues uncovered in today's class. Give everyone a photocopy of the handout. Encourage class members to take time during the coming week to explore the questions and activities listed on the handout.

CLOSING

Taking It Home

(up to 5 minutes)

Form pairs and have partners take turns answering the following questions. Ask:

● **How will you live out the message of today's lesson during the next week?** (Spend five minutes a day worshiping God; read my Bible each day; spend time with others from church; help out a non-Christian friend.)

● **How can you use what you've learned today to find your place in the church?** (I can help create worship services that are biblical and meaningful; I can volunteer at our church's shelter for the homeless.)

Let partners spend a moment in prayer encouraging one another to apply their answers to this question.

After the prayers, say: **I'd like you to exchange phone numbers with your partner. Sometime during this week, give your partner a call and ask how successful he or she has been keeping this commitment.**

Have everyone stand as you dismiss with this blessing: **May our Lord Jesus Christ give us the wisdom and the courage ▶ to work toward a balanced, healthy church that honors God. Amen.**

 ◀ **THE POINT**

🕐 For Extra Time

CHURCH PLANTING

(up to 10 minutes)

Form trios and give each trio a sheet of paper and a pencil. Tell the trios to imagine they've been given the task of planting a new church in your community. Instruct them to create plans for structuring churches that balance worship, instruction, community, and outreach. Encourage the trios to give specific details explaining how their programs would relate to one or more of the four elements.

HERE AT HOME
(up to 10 minutes)

Have class members name every program, committee, or activity in your church. As they call out names, write them on a sheet of newsprint. Then correlate each of these with one or more of the four elements of a healthy church. On the basis of your analysis, evaluate how well your church balances worship, instruction, community, and outreach.

■ Planning-Committee Scriptures

GROUP 1

1. Read each Scripture listed below to discover what it says about worship.
2. Under each biblical reference, record what the Bible teaches about worship.
   ● Psalm 113

   ● John 4:23-24

   ● Romans 12:1

   ● Philippians 4:6-7

GROUP 2

1. Read each Scripture listed below to discover what it says about instruction.
2. Under each biblical reference, record what the Bible teaches about instruction.
   ● Deuteronomy 6:4-9

   ● John 14:26

   ● Colossians 3:16

   ● 2 Timothy 3:16–4:2

GROUP 3

1. Read each Scripture listed below to discover what it says about community.
2. Under each biblical reference, record what the Bible teaches about community.
   ● Romans 12:9-16

   ● Galatians 6:2

   ● Ephesians 2:13-22

   ● James 5:13-16

GROUP 4

1. Read each Scripture listed below to discover what it says about outreach.
2. Under each biblical reference, record what the Bible teaches about outreach.
   ● Matthew 28:18-20

   ● Acts 1:8

   ● James 1:26-27

   ● 1 Peter 3:15-16

A Healthy Balance

APPLY■IT■TO
LIFE
THIS WEEK

The Point: ▶ Healthy churches balance worship, instruction, community, and outreach.

Scripture Focus: Acts 2:42-47

Reflecting on God's Word

Each day this week, read one of the following Scriptures and examine what it says about the characteristics of a healthy church. Then examine how well you are applying the message of that passage in your life. List your discoveries in the space under each passage.

Day 1: Revelation 2:1-7. We must not lose our first love for Christ.

Day 2: Revelation 2:8-17. We must remain strong during times of trial.

Day 3: Revelation 2:18-29. We must guard against false teachers.

Day 4: Revelation 3:1-6. We must not allow ourselves to become spiritually dead.

Day 5: Revelation 3:7-13. We must wait for God's deliverance.

Day 6: Revelation 3:14-22. We must repent when God disciplines us.

Beyond Reflection

Going to Church This Week?
Nearly one half (42 percent) of American adults attend church every week.

---

1. Consider the statistic in the box above and answer these questions:
● Why do you think so many adults attend church?
● Why do you or don't you attend church regularly?
● What effect do you think church attendance has on society as a whole?

2. Spend four days exploring The Point of this lesson.
● On the first day, spend 30 minutes in worship. For example, you might sing worship songs, pray, or thankfully enjoy the good things God has given you.
● On the second day, spend 30 minutes in instruction. For example, you might read a book about a religious topic of interest, listen to a tape of your pastor's last sermon, or attend a Bible study.
● On the third day, spend 30 minutes building community in your church. For example, you might send cards to others in your class or take a church friend out to lunch.
● On the fourth day, spend 30 minutes reaching out to others. For example, you might spend time at a shelter for the homeless, pray for non-Christian friends, or make an appointment to tell someone about your faith.
● After the fourth day, record your thoughts and observations from your experience. Then share your observations with others in your class.

Next Week's Bible Passages: Romans 12:3-8 and 1 Corinthians 12:12-26

Together We Stand

Everyone contributes something important to the church.   ◀ **THE POINT**

Participants will
- discuss the benefits of diversity in the church,
- explore what their spiritual gifts might be, and
- encourage each other to use their gifts and talents.

BIBLE BASIS

Look up the Scriptures for this lesson. Then read the following background paragraphs to see how the passages relate to people today.

Romans 12:3-8 teaches that we are equal before God but serve one another with diverse gifts of the Spirit.

ROMANS 12:3-8

Paul's letter to the Romans presents an exhaustive explanation of the gospel. However, Romans is more than a treatise on sin and forgiveness. Paul knew that people also need help understanding how to live as Christians.

Romans 12:1-2 states the basic requirement of the Christian life: We should all present ourselves to God, then be changed from the inside out by altering the way we think. But Paul doesn't expect us all to think and act in exactly the same way. Romans 12:3-8 teaches that each of us has specific responsibilities to God and to one another. To meet those responsibilities, we must know exactly who we are. We shouldn't think too highly of ourselves or belittle ourselves. On the contrary, Paul wants us to have "sensible" or "reasonable" (Greek *sōphroneō*) opinions of ourselves.

We also need to understand who we are as members of

the church. The parts of a human body are equal but different. In the same way, the members of Christ's body are equal even though each person performs a different role. Also, just as a physical body is at its best when every part does what God intended it to do, Christ's body performs most effectively when each person in it does what God has equipped him or her to do. In sum, though we're all different from one another, we still need each other.

Consequently, we shouldn't worry about our position or status in the church. God has enabled different people to perform different functions, and no one is more important than anyone else. God wants us to discover our gifts and to use that spiritual giftedness to serve others.

1 CORINTHIANS 12:12-26

In **1 Corinthians 12:12-26**, Paul discusses the unity of the church and the diversity of its members.

The church at the Greek city of Corinth struggled with various sins and false teachings. However, the church's primary problem—the one that was at the root of many others—was disunity. In fact, the church members disagreed so much that even good things in their midst began to sour.

For example, the Corinthians used the gifts of the Spirit not to serve and help one another, but to compete with one another. This revealed a total misunderstanding of the nature and purpose of the gifts. In 1 Corinthians 12-14, Paul corrects their distorted views.

As in Romans 12, Paul encourages his readers to think of the church as a body. A physical body is a unity, though it is made up of many different parts. In the same way, the church (Christ's body) is a unity, though it is comprised of many different people. The Holy Spirit unites Christians into one unified body regardless of their ethnic heritage (Jew or non-Jew) or social standing (slave or free).

Since diversity is essential to our unity, it's absurd to think that we should all be exactly alike or that some are more important than others. In the first place, a body comprised of only an eye or an ear wouldn't be a body at all. It'd be a monstrosity. In addition, no part of the body can casually dispense with the others. On the contrary, the body provides special protection to its more vulnerable parts (the internal organs) and modestly clothes parts that need covering (the sexual organs). How much more, Paul implies, should the church body protect its weaker members and cover those who generally don't receive recognition with special honor?

Simply put, both the physical body and the church body need diversity and unity. Diversity produces strength, adaptability, and health, while unity guarantees that all parts work together for the good of the whole.

Imagine what might've happened if the Apostle Paul had said, "I'm tired of preaching. I'm sick of traveling. That's it. I'm sure I've fulfilled my obligation to the church. I think I'll take the next 20 years off."

Sound ridiculous? Unfortunately, that's the attitude of many Christians today. Apathy, busyness, and insecurity often prevent Christians from making vital contributions to their churches. But the Bible tells us that Christians *must* work together, using God's gifts to extend God's kingdom into the world. Use this lesson to help class members discover the importance of their contributions to the church.

THIS LESSON AT A GLANCE

Section	Minutes	What Participants Will Do	Supplies
OPENING	up to 10	**MUST READ**—Name the one book (besides the Bible) they think everyone should read and why.	
BIBLE EXPLORATION AND APPLICATION	20 to 30	☐ *Option 1:* **VARIETY**—Form groups based on different interests and discuss 1 Corinthians 12:12-26.	Bibles
	15 to 20	☐ *Option 2:* **SPIRITUAL-GIFTS INVENTORY**—Discuss Romans 12:6-8 after using a handout to indicate possible gifts and abilities.	Bibles, "Spiritual-Gifts Indicator" handout (p. 49), pencils
CLOSING	up to 5	**TOOLBOX AFFIRMATIONS**—Encourage each other with positive comparisons to tools in a toolbox.	Toolbox filled with tools
FOR EXTRA TIME	up to 10	**OTHER GIFTS**—Create spiritual-gifts inventories from 1 Corinthians 12:4-11, 27-31; Ephesians 4:7-13; and 1 Peter 4:10-11.	Bibles, paper, pencils
	up to 5	**CHURCH SPLIT**—Discuss why churches split and think of ways to prevent or heal a church split.	

Must Read

(up to 10 minutes)

Begin this class session by saying: **Welcome to the third week of our study of the church. So far we've learned that the church finds its life and power in the Holy Spirit and that healthy churches balance worship, instruction, community, and outreach. Today we want to examine the role of the individual in the church. In short, together we're going to explore how**  **everyone contributes something important to the church.**

Encourage class members to get involved in the discussions and activities during the study.

Say: **Think for a moment about your favorite books. Now think about this question: If you could recommend only one book—other than the Bible—for everyone in the world to read, what would that book be and why?**

Allow everyone a minute or two to think about the question, then let class members compare their answers. When everyone has responded, form trios and have them discuss the following questions. Ask:

● **How are the members of our group like diverse books in a library?** (Both cover a wide range of interests; each book or person makes a unique contribution; there's strength in numbers with both books and people.)

● **What are the benefits of diversity in the church? What are the drawbacks?** (We can help each other grow in different ways; we can learn from people with different perspectives; sometimes diversity makes it hard to communicate clearly.)

● **What would the church be like if everyone in it were exactly the same?** (The same as a library with only one book; boring; out of touch with humanity; limited.)

Say: **Just as a library needs many different books to be useful, a church needs many different people to be effective. Let's explore how** ▷ **everyone contributes something important to the church.**

T H E   P O I N T ▷

TEACHER TIP

If you prefer, suggest that class members name their favorite movies or TV shows.

T H E   P O I N T ▷

BIBLE EXPLORATION AND APPLICATION

☐ **OPTION 1:**

Variety

(20 to 30 minutes)

Say: **The object of this next activity is to form groups of four or five based on criteria that I'll give you in a moment. Remember, to do** this you'll need to move around and talk with lots of other people.

Here are the criteria. Each of your group members
● **must be someone not related to you,**
● **must have a hobby different from yours,**
● **must have a religious background different from yours, and**
● **must have a talent or ability different from yours.**

After about five minutes (or when groups are formed), call time. Instruct anyone who hasn't found a group to join the three or four people closest to him or her. Ask a volunteer from each group to describe how completely the members met (or didn't meet) the criteria you established.

Then instruct groups to discuss the following questions. After each question, ask volunteers to share their groups' insights with the rest of the class. Ask:

● **How easy was it to find people who met the different criteria?** (It was easy to find people with different hobbies; it was hard to find people from different religious backgrounds; it was easy to find people who have different abilities.)

● **What does this activity tell you about our class?** (We have many different strengths; we're not very religiously diverse; our members have a variety of interests.)

● **How does our class compare with the early church?** (They were probably as diverse as we are; many of them were new Christians, so they were all starting from the same place.)

● **Was it easy to tell other people about yourself? Why or why not?** (It was hard because I was afraid I was the only new Christian; since we were all sharing, it was relatively easy; it was hard until I discovered that people were interested in my special abilities.)

● **How might your group members contribute to your life? to your spiritual growth?** (Those with older kids could teach me about parenting; they could be with me during difficult times; they could teach me from their experiences.)

● **How could you contribute to the lives of your group members? to their spiritual growth?** (I could take them meals when they're ill; I could show them how to repair their cars; I could encourage and pray for them.)

Say: **Christians in the early church were just as diverse as we are. They, too, had different interests and abilities and came from different backgrounds. But diversity was never an excuse to avoid working together or building up one another. Read 1 Corinthians 12:12-26 in your groups and then we'll discuss it together.**

TEACHER **TIP**

Write the criteria on newsprint or a blackboard so people can refer to them easily. Mingle with the class and encourage everyone to interact with others.

THE POINT ▷

After groups read the Scripture, ask the following questions. Allow groups to discuss each one before reporting their insights to the whole class. Ask:

● **According to verses 12-14, what is the basis of unity in the church? What things are not the basis of unity?** (We're all members of Christ's body; the Holy Spirit creates unity; unity isn't based on externals such as racial or social similarity.)

● **In your opinion, how does the Holy Spirit produce unity in the church?** (By using our diverse abilities for the common good; through the use of the spiritual gifts; by negating external things that divide us.)

● **How can we encourage unity without demanding uniformity?** (We can welcome people who are different from us into our group; we can recognize each person's unique contributions; we can focus everyone's attention on our common goal.)

● **According to 1 Corinthians 12:15-26, how is the church body like a human body? How is it different?** (Both the parts of a body and the members of a church need each other; both bodies need different components to function effectively; it's easier to see how the parts of a body are supposed to work together.)

● **How well does our church reflect the truths of this passage?** (We're unified, but only because we're all alike; everyone makes a unique and important contribution; we're divided—some people think that they're more important than others.)

● **How can we implement Paul's teachings even more fully?** (We can remind each person of his or her importance to the group; we can use our gifts and abilities to serve others; we can spend more time with people who are different from us.)

Say: **According to Paul, diversity in the church is more than a nice idea. It's an essential part of healthy church life. Sometimes it's easy to forget that ▷ everyone contributes something important to the church. But as we've discovered, even in this group we have a wonderful diversity of gifts and abilities to do the work of the church.**

■ ■

FOR *Even Deeper* DISCUSSION

Form groups of four or fewer and discuss the following questions:

● What are the "weaker" body parts (1 Corinthians 12:22)? the "less honorable" (1 Corinthians 12:23)? What are the weaker parts of the church body? the less honorable? How does God give "greater honor" to those parts that lack it (1 Corinthians 12:24)?

● Paul teaches in 1 Corinthians 12:13 that our unity in the Holy Spirit supersedes human divisions. Should our church be more racially diverse? Why or why not? Should our church be more socially diverse? Why or why not?

■■■■■■■■■■■■■■■■■■■■■■■■■■■■■

□ O P T I O N 2 :
Spiritual-Gifts Inventory
(15 to 20 minutes)

Before class, make one copy of the "Spiritual-Gifts Indicator" handout (p. 49) for each person.

Say: ▶ **Everyone contributes something important to the church because God has given each one of us a different ability to serve other Christians. We call these special abilities "spiritual gifts." Paul talks about these gifts and how we should use them in Romans 12:3-8.**

Form pairs and instruct them to read **Romans 12:3-8.** After everyone is finished reading, tell pairs to discuss the following questions. After each question, ask volunteers to report their pairs' answers. Encourage everyone to ask for clarification about anything that may not be clear. Ask:

● **In light of Romans 12:3-8, how would you define "spiritual gift"?** (It's a special ability to serve other people; it's a God-given capability to help others; it's a talent God gives a person to build up the body of Christ.)

● **Does this passage imply that every Christian has a spiritual gift? Explain.** (Yes, God created every body part to do something, and God equips every Christian to perform some task; yes, God has given every Christian the grace to do something.)

● **According to Paul, what's the purpose of spiritual gifts?** (They're supposed to serve the body; we should help others with our spiritual gifts; we're supposed to serve one another with them.)

● **What should our attitude be when we use a spiritual gift?** (We should be realistic about our abilities; we shouldn't be arrogant or conceited; we should focus on serving others instead of ourselves.)

● **What prevents us from using our spiritual gifts as effectively as we could?** (We don't know what our spiritual gifts are; we feel that our spiritual gifts aren't important; we're afraid to fail.)

Say: **Since each one of us has a spiritual gift, ▶ each one of us can make an important contribution to the**

◀ **T H E P O I N T**

T E A C H E R
TIP

To help people define "spiritual gift," ask them to explain how to tell if a "gift" is spiritual or not. For example, is it accurate to say that someone has the spiritual gift of leadership when he or she displayed leadership abilities prior to becoming a Christian? Does God turn natural abilities into spiritual gifts? Is the way we use a gift what determines whether or not it's spiritual?

◀ **T H E P O I N T**

church. So let's discover how we can contribute to the lives and spiritual growth of people in our group.

Give each person a copy of the "Spiritual-Gifts Indicator" handout and a pencil.

Say: **This handout will help you discover which gifts you might possess. Take several minutes to silently complete your handout. We'll discuss these in pairs when we're done.**

Give people five to seven minutes to work on their handouts. Encourage people to complete the questions and identify one or more areas of giftedness. Then instruct class members to re-form their original pairs and discuss the following questions. Ask pairs to report their answers after each question. Ask:

● **What did you learn about the spiritual gifts by completing this handout?** (There are a lot of different ways to serve; I don't understand the gifts as well as I'd like; everyone can do at least some of the things listed.)

● **What did you learn about your own spiritual gifts?** (Although I'm a new Christian, I can show understanding to others; God can use my experiences to encourage others; my gift is exactly what some in the group need.)

● **What does this reveal about the diversity of spiritual gifts in our group?** (We have the ability to meet all of each other's needs; at least one person has each of the gifts; God has given us everything we need to be healthy and effective.)

● **What would our group be like if only a few people had gifts or used their gifts?** (We'd become unbalanced; people would leave for groups where they could get their needs met; as a body, we'd be unhealthy and weak.)

● **How can you serve others with your spiritual gift this week?** (I can ask God each day to give me one person to show mercy to; I can call and encourage one friend who's struggling with life; I can offer to teach a Bible study.)

T H E   P O I N T ▷

Say: **Romans 12:3-8 teaches that** ▷ **every Christian contributes something important to the church. We all need each other. You're important because only you can use your gifts the way God intended, but others are equally as important to you. Let's make sure that we all work together for God's glory and our good by serving each other with our own particular spiritual gifts.**

■ ■

FOR *Even Deeper*
DISCUSSION

Form groups of four or fewer and discuss the following questions:

● The Bible gives different lists of spiritual gifts. Do you think there are other spiritual gifts that the Bible doesn't mention? How can we tell if a particular ability is a spiritual gift or not?

● Are all of the spiritual gifts that the Bible mentions available today? Should every spiritual gift be practiced at every church?

● What's the difference between a spiritual gift and a talent? To what extent does God use or transform our talents into spiritual gifts?

■ ■

APPLY■IT■TO
LIFE
THIS WEEK The "Apply-It-To-Life This Week" handout (p. 50) helps people further explore the issues uncovered in today's class. Give everyone a photocopy of the handout. Encourage class members to take time during the coming week to explore the questions and activities listed on the handout.

CLOSING

Toolbox Affirmations

(up to 5 minutes)

Show everyone a toolbox filled with construction tools and say: **In many ways, a church is like God's toolbox, and its members are God's tools. Let's take a moment to encourage each other as God's tools, working together to build God's kingdom in our church and in our world.**

Form groups of no more than four and give each group a tool from the toolbox. Have adults take turns completing this sentence about each other, inserting a name, a type of tool, and a positive quality of that person: "*(Name)*, as a *(tool)* builds a house, you build up our church with *(a positive quality)*."

For example, someone could say, "Sarah, as a hammer builds a house, you build up our church with your leadership skills" or "Eric, as a saw builds a house, you build up our church with your sharp intellect."

When groups finish, dismiss with a prayer such as this: **Lord, thank you for showing us how ▷ everyone contributes something important to the church. Help us all to be tools in the hands of the Master as we use our gifts this week. Amen.**

TEACHER
TIP

Be sure tools are clean and don't have any jagged edges that may cut people or tear their clothing.

◁ **THE POINT**

For Extra Time

OTHER GIFTS

(up to 10 minutes)

Form groups of three. Assign each group either 1 Corinthians 12:4-11, 27-31; Ephesians 4:7-13; or 1 Peter 4:10-11. Instruct trios to read their passages and create their own spiritual-gifts inventories. Encourage group members to think of ways these gifts are expressed today and formulate those into statements for the inventories. Ask groups to share their inventories with each other when they're done.

CHURCH SPLIT

(up to 5 minutes)

Form groups of four and have groups discuss the phenomenon of church splits. Have groups answer the following questions. Ask volunteers to report their groups' discoveries after each question. Ask:

● What kinds of conflicts often cause churches to break apart?

● How can churches solve those conflicts before they lead to a split?

● How can Christians promote healing after a church split?

SPIRITUAL-GIFTS INDICATOR

This spiritual-gifts indicator is based on the gifts listed in Romans 12:6-8. Other spiritual gifts are listed in 1 Corinthians 12:4-11, 27-31; Ephesians 4:7-13; and 1 Peter 4:10-11.

Read each of the following statements and determine how well it describes you. Mark the statements according to the following scale:

M=This describes me **most** of the time.
S=This describes me **sometimes.**
N=This does **not** really describe me.

_____1. I look for creative ways to meet others' needs.
_____2. People generally look to me to make the first move.
_____3. I try hard to help others feel good about themselves.
_____4. Teaching a Sunday school class or Bible study interests me.
_____5. I'm likely to mow a neighbor's lawn or take a meal to someone who's been sick.
_____6. I'm drawn to people others might consider "outcasts."
_____7. I'm likely to notice when those around me are feeling down.
_____8. I like the idea of sharing what God has told me with others.
_____9. Giving is an important part of my financial plan.
_____10. I'm likely to generate enthusiasm among others.
_____11. When I lend things, I don't worry about getting them back.
_____12. Others tell me I explain things in a clear, easy-to-understand way.
_____13. I appreciate what others do, and I tell them so.
_____14. I feel called to tell others what God reveals to me.
_____15. I'm not bothered when my work goes unnoticed.
_____16. People who need help solving problems often ask for my opinion.
_____17. I think everyone deserves second and third chances.
_____18. I enjoy preparing lessons because I like sharing what I learn with others.
_____19. I'm interested in ministering to prisoners, the homeless, the disabled, and people in similar situations.
_____20. People tell me I present biblical messages in a clear, compelling way.
_____21. I'm likely to volunteer for tasks others may have neglected.

Each statement describes a possible demonstration of a spiritual gift. Statements you marked with an M could indicate giftedness in the corresponding spiritual gift. Two or more related statements marked with an S could also indicate giftedness.

Match your responses with the gifts below by circling the statement numbers that you ranked with an M. Those qualities with the most M rankings are probably your spiritual gifts.

- prophecy: 8, 14, 20
- serving: 5, 15, 21
- teaching: 4, 12, 18
- showing mercy: 6, 17, 19
- encouraging: 3, 7, 13
- giving: 1, 9, 11
- leading: 2, 10, 16

Together We Stand

The Point: ▶ Everyone contributes something important to the church.

Scripture Focus: Romans 12:3-8 and 1 Corinthians 12:12-26

Reflecting on God's Word

Each day this week, read one of the following Scriptures and examine what it says about working together. Then examine how well you are applying the message of the passage in your life. List your discoveries in the space under each passage.

Day 1: Acts 6:1-7. The early church makes sure everyone is treated fairly.

Day 2: James 2:1-13. We shouldn't show favoritism in the church.

Day 3: Ecclesiastes 4:9-12. Two people are safer and stronger than one.

Day 4: Philippians 2:1-11. We should imitate Christ's example of humility.

Day 5: Ephesians 4:1-13. God gives diverse gifts to promote unity in the body.

Day 6: Romans 14:13–15:4. We should limit our rights in order to build up others.

Pointless Study?

"It is pointless to study the subject of grace [spiritual] gifts if we have no intention of exercising them."
—Dr. Norm Wakefield

Beyond Reflection

1. Read the quote by Dr. Norm Wakefield in the box above. Then think about these questions:
- Do you agree or disagree with the statement? Why?
- What happens when a person studies spiritual gifts but then doesn't exercise them?
- How will you exercise your gifts this week?

2. Think of your three closest Christian friends. What spiritual gifts do you see at work in their lives? Give each of them something that represents your appreciation for the way they use their spiritual gifts.

For example, you might give an encouraging friend a T-shirt with the logo of a championship team to let that person know he or she is a winner. You could give a coupon good for one free carwash at your house to a friend who often displays a gift of serving.

Make it a goal to give your gifts this week.

Next Week's Bible Passages: Acts 15:1-21 and Galatians 5:13-15

Divided We Fall

God can help us resolve conflict in a positive way.

◀ T H E   P O I N T

OBJECTIVES

Participants will
- discover the diversity within the class,
- learn and apply biblical principles for resolving conflict, and
- work from different perspectives to solve an early church conflict.

BIBLE BASIS

Look up the Scriptures for this lesson. Then read the following background paragraphs to see how the passages relate to people today.

Acts 15:1-21 records a meeting of early church leaders at Jerusalem.

ACTS 15:1-21

During its first decade, the church was almost entirely Jewish. Jesus was a Jew, and all the members of the early church were either Jews, non-Jews who had converted to Judaism through circumcision and obedience to the law of Moses (proselytes), or non-Jews who followed the Jewish God and his moral law (God-fearers). Eventually, however, God's Spirit motivated some Jewish Christians to share the gospel with others who had no connection with Judaism. Acts 15 describes the conflict that this free offer of the gospel created.

The problem surfaced when Jewish Christians from Judea went to Antioch and told the non-Jewish Christians there that they had to be circumcised and obey the law of Moses. In short, they were teaching that people had to be or become Jews before they could become Christians. Paul and Barnabas disagreed, and eventually the two sides took the dispute to the church leaders at Jerusalem.

Those who wanted to maintain Christianity's Jewish

focus restated their demand for circumcision and Moses' law. But Peter reminded everyone that God had commissioned him to take the gospel to non-Jews. In addition, God had sent his Spirit to non-Jewish Christians who didn't obey the Mosaic law.

After Paul and Barnabas recounted their experiences, James—Jesus' brother and the leader of the Jerusalem church—announced his decision. Since God had always wanted non-Jews to seek him, James didn't want to make it difficult for them to turn to God. He said they didn't have to be circumcised or obey the Law. James asked only that non-Jewish Christians avoid certain practices that would keep Jewish Christians from enjoying fellowship with them (see Acts 15:20).

The Jerusalem council is a model for handling conflict in the church. Instead of backbiting, politicking, or threatening to divide the church, early Christians combined open communication, mutual respect, and God's leading to reach a fair and acceptable solution. We can do the same to resolve church conflicts today.

GALATIANS 5:13-15

Galatians 5:13-15 teaches that we are free from the Law but not from our responsibility to love one another.

The question addressed in Acts 15:1-21 also plagued the churches of Galatia, a region in Asia Minor. After Paul established those churches, certain Jewish Christians came along and taught that non-Jewish people who wanted to become Christians had to be circumcised and obey Moses' law. Paul responds to this attack on the gospel, refuting it in his letter to the Galatians.

Paul devotes most of Galatians to the defense of the gospel. However, he shifts to a new topic in Galatians 5:13. After summarizing his argument ("You...were called to be free"), Paul warns the Galatians against misusing freedom as an "opportunity for self-indulgence" (New Revised Standard Version). The Greek word for opportunity *(aphormē)* sometimes refers to a military base of operations, so Paul may mean that Christians shouldn't allow freedom to be a base of attack. Rather, we should continually serve each other in love. When we do this, we fully obey the Law, which can be reduced to the single command of Leviticus 19:18—Love your neighbor as yourself.

Loving one another pleases God and serves our own interests. Christians who fight are like wild animals who bite *(daknō)*, devour *(katesthiō)*, and often destroy each other. Even in the church, unrestrained conflict guarantees destruction. According to Paul, the only way we can avoid destruction is to serve one another in love.

People in many churches argue over just about anything. They fight over the color of the carpet in the sanctuary, the amount of money allocated to the youth budget, and the length of the Sunday sermon. They take sides over the style of music appropriate for church, the pastor's responsibilities, and the correct views on various doctrinal and social issues.

Conflict handled in an inappropriate way can lead to hurt feelings, power struggles, a sense of abandonment, and even a church split. Yet conflict in a church isn't always bad. In fact, it may be a sign of a healthy, growing body of Christians. Use this lesson to help your class members understand how they can turn conflict in the church into an opportunity to strengthen the body of Christ.

THIS LESSON AT A GLANCE

Section	Minutes	What Participants Will Do	Supplies
OPENING	*up to 5*	**CHURCH SONGS**—Choose song titles that describe their experiences with church.	
BIBLE EXPLORATION AND APPLICATION	*15 to 20*	☐ *Option 1:* **INSIGNIFICANT WARS**—Debate a church-related issue, then discuss Galatians 5:13-15 to discover how to resolve conflicts in the church.	Bibles
	20 to 30	☐ *Option 2:* **PROBLEMS OF THE PAST**—Propose solutions to an early-church problem, then learn principles of conflict resolution from Acts 15:1-21.	Bibles, "The Jerusalem Council" handout (p. 61), pencils
CLOSING	*up to 5*	**TOGETHER WE STAND**—Stand in unison as a symbol of their desire to work together to solve conflict.	
FOR EXTRA TIME	*up to 10*	**FIGHT ABOUT WHAT?**—List areas of frequent conflict in the church, then discuss how to solve conflicts in those areas.	
	up to 10	**COURSE REFLECTION**—Complete sentences to describe what they've learned from this course.	

Church Songs

(up to 5 minutes)

To begin class, say: **Last week we discovered that God uses our diverse gifts and abilities to build a strong and healthy church body. But sometimes we're not even aware of our differences and how they affect our relationships. Let me show you what I mean.**

Form groups of three or fewer, then say: **Think for a moment about how your experiences have shaped your attitudes toward the church.** Pause. **Now think about this question: If you were to assign a song title to those experiences, which song title would you choose?**

For example, if you've moved from church to church, your song might be "On the Road Again." Or, if you've always relied on the church, you might choose "Great is Thy Faithfulness."

When everyone has had a moment to think, have trio members tell each other their song titles and explain why they chose those titles. Then let members report their song titles to the entire class. For even more fun, encourage anyone who is brave enough to sing a line from his or her song.

THE POINT ▷

Say: **We all come from different backgrounds, and conflict is inevitable with people as diverse as we are. But that's OK because ▷ God can help us resolve conflict in a positive way. Let's ask God to be with us as we study conflict in the church and how to resolve it productively.**

Have trios spend a moment praying, silently or aloud, for God to teach them during the lesson.

TEACHER TIP

If none of the statements are likely to provoke appropriate debate, write your own statement or reword one of the given statements to fit your group. For example, you might say, "The church shouldn't take sides on social or political issues," or "We should allocate as much money to missionaries as we do to the church staff." You may also want to prearrange for two spirited class members to take opposing sides during the debate.

BIBLE EXPLORATION AND APPLICATION

☐ **OPTION 1:**

Insignificant Wars

(15 to 20 minutes)

Before class choose one of the following statements for discussion. Select a statement that will provoke some debate among your class members, but avoid any topic that might create a heated discussion or a hostile atmosphere. The activity is designed to lead people to think about conflict resolution by experiencing a *minor* disagreement.

● We should structure our church services to attract non-Christians.

● The pastor's main responsibility is to preach and

teach the Bible.

- The church should give as much money to the poor as it does to missionaries.

- We should sing more contemporary songs than old, traditional hymns.

- The church should take clear, public stands on the social and moral issues of our day.

- We should base our church budget on need (not anticipated giving) and trust God to provide the funds.

Read the statement to the entire class and ask for their responses. Encourage participants to state their positions clearly and to explain why they support those positions. Allow at least five minutes for discussion, then form trios. Instruct trios to discuss the following questions among themselves, then have volunteers report their trios' responses after each question. Ask:

- **What were you thinking during our discussion?** (I was afraid the debate would get out of hand; I was disappointed people wouldn't agree with me; it doesn't take much to start an argument at church.)

- **Why do we hold different opinions on this issue?** (We all have different backgrounds and interests; we all have different opinions about the biblical teaching on this issue.)

- **How important is the issue we discussed?** (It's something I won't compromise on; it's just a matter of personal preference; it's worth debating, but not worth dividing over.)

- **How was our discussion like serious conflicts within the church? How is it different?** (The longer we debated, the harder it was to agree; we lost sight of the important issues; this discussion was much friendlier.)

- **How is the way people responded during our discussion similar to the way we handle church conflicts?** (Sometimes we argue about minor details; we assume others will speak up for our viewpoints; we're sometimes quick to speak and slow to listen.)

Instruct trios to read **Galatians 5:13-15.** Then ask:

- **How do we indulge our sinful natures during conflicts?** (We try to make the other side look bad; we become self-righteous; we focus on winning instead of on discovering the truth.)

- **In what ways can we lovingly serve people we disagree with?** (We can respectfully listen to their opinions; we can recognize the valid parts of their ideas; we can deepen our relationships in areas where we do agree.)

- **What potential conflicts does our church face?** (In two weeks we'll discuss the annual budget; some new members want to change the format of the Sunday morning service.)

TEACHER
TIP

If your statement doesn't provoke adequate debate, state your opinion and ask people to respond to it or play "devil's advocate" by disagreeing with people who have already given their opinions. Or, you may want to choose another statement and have people respond to it.

● **What might create conflict in these situations?** (Considering only our own interests; reacting emotionally instead of thoughtfully; refusing to talk things through with those who disagree with us.)

● **How can we use the teachings of Galatians 5:13-15 to avoid conflict in those situations?** (We can encourage people to respect one another's ideas and opinions; we can try to do what's best for the group as a whole; we can commit to serving others instead of ourselves.)

Say: **Conflict is rarely pleasant, but it doesn't have to destroy our relationships. Galatians 5:13-15 teaches us how ▶ God can help us resolve conflict in a positive way. Let's remember the principles it teaches and apply them the next time a conflict arises in our church.**

T H E   P O I N T ▷

■■■■■■■■■■■■■■■■■■■■■■■■■■■■■■■

FOR *Even Deeper*
DISCUSSION

Form groups of four or fewer and discuss the following questions:

● In Galatians 1:6-10, Paul pronounces condemnation on anyone who disagrees with his teaching on the gospel. When might conflict be God's will? How can God use conflict to accomplish something positive? How can we know when we should fight and when we should compromise?

● What does it mean to "love" someone? How should love affect the way we respond to those we have conflicts with? When, if ever, should love motivate us to create conflict?

■■■■■■■■■■■■■■■■■■■■■■■■■■■■■

☐ O P T I O N   2 :
*Problems of
the Past*
(20 to 30 minutes)

Before class make one photocopy of the "Jerusalem Council" handout (p. 61) for each class member.

Ask the class to form trios. (If you completed the previous activity, form new trios.) Instruct trio members to number off from one to three.

Then say: **Acts 15 describes a church council in Jerusalem at which two groups debated the status of non-Jewish Christians. Let's imagine for a moment that we're delegates to this council and we have to decide how to resolve this conflict.**

Instruct class members to read **Acts 15:1-12** within their groups and answer the following question:

● **What's the basic question that we must answer?**

(Must non-Jewish Christians obey the law of Moses? Must a person become a Jew before he or she can become a Christian?)

Ask volunteers to report their trios' answers, then send the ones, twos, and threes to different areas of the room. Give each person a copy of the "Jerusalem Council" handout and a pencil.

Then say: **Now that we know what the conflict is about, let's see how successful we are at resolving it. Ones, you're with Paul, Barnabas, and Peter. You're convinced that non-Jewish Christians should be left alone and not forced to adhere to Jewish customs.**

Twos, you're Christians who are steeped in the tradition of the Pharisees. You regard faith in Christ as a continuation of the Jewish faith. So you're convinced that all Christians, whether Jewish or not, must follow the Jewish religious customs.

Threes, you belong to James' group of apostles and elders. You haven't taken either side yet, but you're committed to resolving this conflict quickly and fairly.

Work with your group members to complete your section of the handout. In about 10 minutes you'll return to your original trio to see how well you and your trio partners can resolve the conflict.

After about 10 minutes, have group members return to their original trios. Instruct trio members to take turns reporting their groups' ideas for solving the conflict. Then have each trio choose a fair and acceptable resolution to the conflict.

When the conflicts have been resolved, have the trios discuss the following questions within their groups. Ask volunteers to report their trios' insights to the rest of the class after each question. Ask:

● **What went through your mind as you worked to resolve this conflict?** (I wanted to resolve the conflict without giving up my desires; I was surprised that this was an issue the early church debated.)

● **What was your response to your trio members' solution?** (I was challenged by their arguments; I was impressed by the variety of ideas; I didn't feel that they were willing enough to compromise.)

● **What was your trio's solution to the conflict?** (We thought both parties should agree to disagree; we decided to form separate groups; we agreed to ignore the requirements of the Law.)

Instruct trios to read **Acts 15:13-21.** Then ask:

● **What was the early church's solution to the problem?** (James decided on a fair compromise; Gentiles didn't have to obey the Law, but they were to respect the

BIBLE INSIGHT

Since Pharisees, unlike Sadducees, accepted the concept of resurrection (Acts 23:6-8), they could become Christians without ceasing to be Pharisees. Many probably retained their devotion to the Law but added to it belief in Jesus and his resurrection. It's likely that they accepted Jesus only after God raised Jesus from the dead and thus vindicated his claim to be the Messiah.

BIBLE INSIGHT

Although non-Jewish Christians didn't have to obey the Law, James encouraged them to be sensitive to Jewish Christians. The practices he asked them to avoid were the same ones that Jewish rabbis asked any non-Jew living among Jews to shun. These practices included any association with idols, eating meat with blood in it, or drinking blood (see Genesis 9:4 and Leviticus 17:10-12). James' reference to "sexual immorality" probably means that non-Jewish Christians weren't to marry people closely related to them (see Leviticus 18:6-18; 1 Corinthians 5:1).

TEACHER TIP

Write the principles of conflict resolution on a sheet of newsprint or a blackboard. If you skipped "Insignificant Wars," instruct trios to read Galatians 5:13-15 and list principles of conflict resolution taught in that passage.

TEACHER TIP

If you didn't complete "Insignificant Wars," have trios discuss the following questions:

- What potential conflicts does our church face?
- How can we apply the principles of Acts 15 to avoid or resolve those conflicts?

T H E   P O I N T ▷

feelings of Jewish Christians.)

- ● **How did our solutions compare to the actual results of the Jerusalem council?** (We came up with similar ideas; our solution leaned toward the Pharisees; we weren't as fair as James was.)

- ● **What principles of conflict resolution can we learn from the council at Jerusalem?** (It's important to allow everyone a chance to speak; after a decision is made, we must put the conflict behind us and move forward together; it's OK to disagree as long as we're not disagreeable.)

- ● **What obstacles make it hard to resolve conflict in a positive way?** (Hurt feelings; unwillingness to compromise; unwillingness to listen to opposing viewpoints; holding grudges.)

- ● **What can we do this week to encourage each other to resolve conflicts in a positive way?** (Remind each other of the example of the early church; ask forgiveness of those we've hurt; open lines of communication with others.)

Say: **As Acts 15 reveals, conflict in the church is nothing new. It's encouraging to see how God resolved church conflict in the past and to know that ▷ God can help us resolve conflict in a positive way, too.**

■ ■

FOR *Even Deeper* DISCUSSION

Form groups of four or fewer and discuss the following questions:

- ● Is the early church's decision that Christians should avoid certain practices offensive to Jews still binding (Acts 15:19-21)? Why or why not? Should we still obey every command in the New Testament? Why or why not?

- ● Should we discuss and decide important issues at church councils today? Why or why not? Which current issues would you like to debate at a church council? Who should be involved in such councils?

■ ■

APPLY■IT■TO **LIFE** THIS WEEK
The "Apply-It-To-Life This Week" handout (p. 62) helps people further explore the issues uncovered in today's class. Give everyone a photocopy of the handout. Encourage class members to take time during the coming week to explore the questions and activities listed on the handout.

Together We Stand

(up to 5 minutes)

Say: **I'm going to call out a few ideas that you may or may not agree with.**

If you agree with the first idea, stand up and remain standing. If not, remain seated. If you like the second idea and you're standing, sit back down. If you like the second idea and you're sitting, stand up. Get it?

Here are the ideas:

● **Chocolate ice cream is superior to vanilla ice cream.**

● **Vacations by the ocean are better than vacations in the mountains.**

● **Watching sports is better than reading a good book.**

● **The chemicals in diet soft drinks are worse than the sugar in regular soft drinks.**

● **Standing is better than sitting.**

At this time, you should have some adults standing and some sitting. Instruct everyone to sit down.

Say: **Even in this brief activity, we discovered many things we disagree about. But I think we can agree that each one of us makes an important contribution to the church. So when disagreements arise, let's remember that** ▶ **God can help us resolve conflicts in a positive way. Let's all stand to signify our togetherness on this issue. Now turn to someone standing nearby and tell that person one thing you'll do to help make your church conflict free.**

◀ **THE POINT**

After a moment close in prayer, thanking God for the ability to handle conflict appropriately.

Before class members leave, thank each person specifically for his or her contribution to the course. Ask class members what they liked most about the course and what they'd like to see different about it. Please note their comments (along with your own) and send them to the Adult Curriculum Editor at Group Publishing, Dept. BK, Box 481, Loveland, Colorado 80539. We want your feedback so that we can make each course we publish better than the last. Thanks!

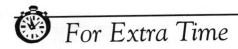 *For Extra Time*

FIGHT ABOUT WHAT?

(up to 10 minutes)

In groups of four or fewer, have people list what church members often fight about. Examples might include use of church resources, budgetary priorities, personnel decisions, doctrinal viewpoints, or change. Then have groups brainstorm ways each type of conflict can be handled to bring about positive results.

COURSE REFLECTION

(up to 10 minutes)

Ask class members to reflect on the past four lessons. Then have them take turns completing the following sentences:

- One thing I learned in this course was...
- If I could tell friends about this course, I'd say...
- One thing I'll do differently because of this course is...

THE JERUSALEM COUNCIL

1 Paul, Barnabas, and Peter

● Read the information in the FYI box below.

> **F.Y.I.** Barnabas and Paul (Saul) had ministered to the mixed (Jewish and non-Jewish) church at Antioch for a full year (Acts 11:22-26). Paul accepted non-Jewish Christians, for God had chosen him to take the good news to non-Jews (Acts 9:15). Finally, God overcame Peter's initial hesitation to embrace non-Jews through direct revelation and personal experience (Acts 10:1-48).

● Using the information in Acts 15:1-12 and the FYI box, briefly outline and defend your position.

● Propose a solution to the conflict.

2 Christians of the Pharisees' Party

● Read the information in the FYI box below.

> **F.Y.I.** Since Pharisees, unlike Sadduccees, accepted the concept of resurrection (Acts 23:6-8), they could become Christians without ceasing to be Pharisees. Many probably retained their devotion to the Law but added to it belief in Jesus and his resurrection.

● Using the information in Acts 15:1-12 and the FYI box, briefly outline and defend your position.

● Propose a solution to the conflict.

3 James, the apostles, and the elders

● Read the information in the FYI box below.

> **F.Y.I.** James was Jesus' brother and the leader of the Jerusalem church (Acts 12:17; 21:18; Galatians 1:19; 2:9). Jewish and Christian historians refer to James as a devout Jew who scrupulously kept the Law and regularly went to the Temple to pray.

● Briefly summarize the issues as you understand them.

● List the steps you would take to resolve the conflict.

Divided We Fall

APPLY ■ IT ■ TO LIFE THIS WEEK

The Point: ▶ God can help us resolve conflict in a positive way.

Scripture Focus: Acts 15:1-21 and Galatians 5:13-15

Reflecting on God's Word

Each day this week, read one of the following Scriptures and think about how it can apply to conflict in church. Then examine how well you are applying the message of the passage in your life. List your discoveries in the space under each passage.

Day 1: Acts 15:36-41. Paul and Barnabas part ways.

Day 2: Matthew 18:15-20. We should restore those who sin against us.

Day 3: James 1:19-21. We shouldn't speak in anger.

Day 4: James 3:13–4:3. Selfishness creates conflict.

Day 5: Matthew 7:1-5. We should judge ourselves first.

Day 6: Matthew 5:23-26. We should be eager to restore peace.

Fact or Fiction?

"Miss Bertha June Biggs had uncanny spiritual sensitivity. She could always tell if something was wrong in the church—even if everyone else thought things were fine."
—From the short story "The Church in Harmony," by John Duckworth

---

Beyond Reflection

1. Read the quotation in the box above and answer these questions:
- What's your initial reaction to the quotation? Why?
- When have you felt like others were stirring up conflicts over minor matters? How did you respond?
- When have you been guilty of having an attitude like Miss Bertha June Biggs? What did you do about it?
- How do you know which issues in the life of a church are worth fighting for?

Consider reading the entire story of "The Church in Harmony," by John Duckworth. You'll find it in his book *Joan 'n' the Whale,* published by Fleming H. Revell Company.

2. Review the "Apply-It-To-Life This Week" handouts from previous lessons. What insights about the church have you gained from your Scripture readings and "Beyond Reflection" activities? Let your class leader know what you've learned and how you've been "applying it to your life."

Fellowship and Outreach Specials

Use the following activities any time you want. You can use them as part of (or in place of) your regular class activities, or you can plan a special event based on one or more of the ideas.

Church Scouts

Compile a list of churches in your community that are willing to let your members observe their ministries. Contact church pastors for permission to do this.

Then form "scout" teams of up to three people who will observe other churches in action on a Sunday morning or evening. Arrange for your scouts to interview church members and pastors afterward. Encourage the scouts to identify strengths that could be incorporated into your church or areas where your church could improve.

Have your teams report their observations and discoveries to your class. For added benefit, invite representatives from other churches to visit and discuss your church's ministries as well.

Church Memories

Help your group members learn more about each other by sharing church memories in a unique way.

Form a circle and give everyone a sheet of paper and a pencil. Ask class members to write for a few minutes about their past church memories. Encourage participants to give details explaining why the memories are meaningful. Also, tell them not to include their names on their papers.

When everyone is finished writing, mix the papers together in a pile. Have one person in the circle choose a paper (other than his or her own) and read aloud the church memory described on it. Then have other group members guess whose memory it is.

Continue around the circle, letting adults take turns choosing and reading church memories until all stories have been read.

Car-Maintenance Day

Recruit the mechanically inclined in your church to reach out to people in your community through a car-maintenance day.

On a designated Saturday, ask volunteers who are knowledgeable about cars to meet at the church and perform simple vehicle maintenance for free. Advertise so that people who need car repairs will bring their cars to the church. Caution your volunteers to do only simple services, thus avoiding the risk of damaging a car. Services might include oil changes, checking and correcting fluid levels, changing spark plugs, changing filters, and inflating tires. Don't accept donations; do this purely as a service to your community.

Provide snacks and drinks for people to enjoy while their cars are being serviced. If you feel it's appropriate, include literature about your church on the table as well. If you get an overwhelming response, you might also consider scheduling appointments so people won't have to wait in long lines.

Block Party

Help your community see the festive side of your church by sponsoring a block party for the neighborhoods nearest your building.

About a week before the party, have church members distribute fliers advertising the block party to homes in the neighborhood. On the day of the party, decorate your church's parking lot or lawn with streamers, balloons, and signs. Play music and provide plenty of food and drinks for everyone to enjoy. Arrange for entertainment such as games or a show. Every 15 minutes or so, give tours of your church. You may want to hand out free balloons to kids and free Bibles to adults.

Canned-Food Rummage Sale

For one month, collect items from church members that they no longer want or need. Make sure you monitor the quality of donated items since they will be used for an all-church rummage sale.

On the day of the rummage sale, display the donated goods in the church parking lot or on the lawn. However, instead of pricing things in dollars and cents, use the barter system and charge your customers canned or non-perishable foods. For example, a children's toy might go for one or two bags of rice, a bicycle might sell for 15 to 20 cans of vegetables, and a refrigerator might be priced at 100 cans of assorted goods.

After the rummage sale, donate all the "proceeds" to the food-distribution agency of your choice.